Joan . Bill Cook.

West Bromwich
in old picture postcards

including Tipton and Wednesbury

Robin Pearson

European Library *ZALTBOMMEL/THE NETHERLANDS*

GB ISBN 90 288 4723 5

© 1988 European Library – Zaltbommel/The Netherlands

Third edition, 2001: reprint of the original edition of 1988.

European Library

post office box 49

NL – 5300 AA Zaltbommel/The Netherlands

telephone: 0031 418 513144

fax: 0031 418 515515

e-mail:publisher@eurobib.nl

INTRODUCTION

In some ways the heyday of the British postcard mirrored the civic pride and satisfaction that West Bromwich felt as a community. From the 1870s onwards the District Hospital was completed, Dartmouth Park laid out, the Oak House was restored and presented by Alderman Reuben Farley whose energy for municipal activity was typical of those who had previously ensured the town achieved borough status and separate parliamentary representation. The Corporation Baths, Law Courts, the West Bromwich Institute, the School of Art and Technical School, the Town Hall, and a newer Public Library were all erected by 1907. A hundred years earlier the population was barely a tenth of that recorded in the 1901 census. It is also perhaps hard to imagine that the town's main street was once a track in the middle of a windswept heath that few people would venture across after dark. Bromwich Heath was carpeted in a kind of heather which is now remembered in the name for part of that area – The Lyng. Bromwich in its earliest uses probably meant the village where the broom grew – the further appellation, West, was added to avoid confusion with two other settlements in Warwickshire, Castle Bromwich and Little Bromwich.

Development after the enclosure of the heath was steady but slow. The novelist David Christie Murray, born in a house on the High Street in 1847, described West Bromwich then as 'a rather doleful hybrid of a place – neither town nor country'. By the time of the publication of his autobiography in 1908 it had become 'a compact business-like town now, and its spreading industries have defaced the lovely fringe of country which used to be around it'.

Although many industries have now died away some manufacturing activities have survived and developed. The spring trade still flourishes in the town. Today we all use without a second thought bathroom and kitchen scales made by Salter's. Apart from its enlightened policy towards its workers this firm achieved a couple of other distinctions – a claim for the production of possibly the first wholly English typewriter, and a works football team, then *The Strollers*, who formed the basis of the future champions West Bromwich Albion.

In 1966 West Bromwich absorbed two of its immediate neighbours in a local government reorganization. One of those places, Tipton, perhaps epitomized more than any other true Black Country town. Even today the ravages of the Industrial Revolution are obvious on its landscape. So much coal was taken out of its ground that by the 1920s the fight to pump water from the mines was lost.

Iron was the other mighty attraction of Tipton for the early industrialists after Dud Dudley was supposedly the first to smelt iron with coal in 1619. Another locally born man, Sir Alfred Hickman, was known as the 'Iron King of the Midlands'. The nineteenth century Bloomfield Ironworks manufactured such a high quality product that it was acknowledged worldwide.

A different kind of fame came to the Horseley Bridge and Engineering Co. Ltd. when it built one of the world's first steam driven iron boats. Many surviving canal bridges are evidence of the company's main work which today's successor firm continues with the construction of motorway bridges.

Another form of bridge had been produced within the boundaries of the third member of the 1966 union. Wednesbury's Patent Shaft made the world's first all-steel bridge erected at Benares over the Ganges in 1885.

It was a different product that had gained renown for Wednesbury as 'tube town' after Cornelius Whitehouse developed a new method of butt welding. James Russell acquired the patent and together with his brother John secured a temporary prosperity for the town. Present-day financial troubles with the loss of Patent Shaft have a familiar ring in an area that has suffered economic depressions both last and earlier this century.

For Wednesbury there was a certain irony in the local government amalgamation since West Bromwich was once part of the Wednesbury Parliamentary District. Apart from the Industrial Revolution all three towns played a significant role in the development of Methodism. Despite the very hostile reception in Wednesbury for John Wesley there was a strong commitment in the town, and neighbouring Tipton was the site for the first meeting house. West Bromwich on the other hand underlines the biblical saying of 'a prophet is not without honour, save in his own country, and in his own house'. In America there was national recognition of Francis Asbury as the 'Prophet of the Long Road' after he had gone there to further Wesley's aims. Not until recently has a postcard been produced locally of his boyhood home on Newton Road.

J.B. Priestley, in his classic 'English Journey', had some harsh words for the Black Country, Wednesbury, and West Bromwich in particular. In his final chapter he did partly redeem the situation by saying that if he were forced to choose between living abroad or in England then he would head straight for West Bromwich!

Acknowledgments
Most of the postcards in this book are from the Sandwell Pictorial Civic Record – in some cases collectors have allowed the library service to copy their originals. Such public spiritedness has permitted a wide range of scenes and views to be shown in this publication. If any individuals have cards not in this book they might like to consider donating them or allowing copies to be made by the library. In either situation such generosity will be acknowledged in the photographic archive.

Thanks to Tony Price of Mitchells & Butlers for the loan of cards 27, 28, 46 and 97.

Many thanks to Patricia Burford and Vanessa Hill respectively present and past members of the staff at the Central Reference Library at West Bromwich; thanks also to Jean Wade for assistance in visiting many of the present day sites of scenes depicted in some of the views; and most of all thanks to John Maddison for the help that he has given in his dual roles as local studies officer for Sandwell and secretary of West Bromwich Civic Pride Association.

WB 12   CHRIST CHURCH AND GARDENS, WEST BROMWICH   A TUCK CARD

1. This view, published by Raphael Tuck & Sons, almost gives an impression of peaceful seclusion that even in 1868 tempted one journalist to describe the main thoroughfare as befitting a smart country town. When he turned off what some claim is England's longest High Street the Black Country was 'faithfully portrayed in every building and every human face'.

LOWER HIGH ST WEST BROMWICH

2. This was the bustling scene behind the photographer in the previous card. Above the two gentlemen in conversation on the corner of Sandwell Road was an office of the auctioneer Thomas Harford, whose company survives as the oldest established firm of estate agents in the town. The adjacent tobacconist was Mrs. Coope who was succeeded by Henry Rotton. A few doors along was an ironmonger's store with Lewis Joseph Evans there for nearly a quarter of a century. At 351 was Martin Magor, the chemist, while his neighbour was Mary Holden, the butcher – unlike today many a woman ran such a business.

3. A party of local blind people and their helpers line up outside the Olympia on the High Street at the start of an outing. Formerly known as the New Hippodrome Music Hall it always presented a mixture of variety and films. The theatre and neighbouring stone masons, the Alexander family who formerly had premises in St. Michael's Street, are now the site occupied by Guest Motors Ltd. Real ale followers will probably be amused by the Whitbread advertisement adjoining Joseph George Tomkins the printer.

4. This Valentine's series card shows a close-up of Highfields, one of the town's larger residences that was not one house but three. The Siddons family, Hill Top industrialists, had the longest stay of its many residents. The building was sold to the Corporation in 1922 but the outbreak of war saved it from demolition in 1939. The Memorial Gardens that now front Highfields were opened in 1951 replacing 'the eyesore of wartime air raid shelters'.

5. Christ Church was built near the new centre of West Bromwich as the turnpike road developed into the High Street. Work began after the laying of the foundation in 1821 but was delayed the next year with the bankruptcy of the builder and the church was finally consecrated in January 1829. The Gothic style seen here in a Wrench series postcard was designed by Francis Goodwin who in 1831 was among architects invited to submit proposals for a new House of Commons. His subsequent plans were described as 'the best' but his determination in 1835 to enter the public competition for the new Houses of Parliament proved too much for his health, with fatal consequences.

6. Christ Church's proximity to Heath Colliery led it to being badly damaged by mining subsidence during the mid-1850s. Restoration was completed in 1858 and again in 1876 after further subsidence. This card shows the church floodlit to celebrate the Michael Faraday Electricity Centenary in September/October 1931. The church was eventually closed in 1975 and demolished in 1980 following a fire. Although the graveyard walks remain with the lime trees planted in 1886 the graves were recently levelled for office re-development on the site.

7. The little boy in this postcard, produced by a local stationer, may well have attended the schoolroom at the rear of the Baptist Church on the opposite side of the High Street to Highfields. The four classrooms could accommodate 350 scholars! The church with its 70 foot tower was built in 1886 opening in May of the following year; the total cost including land was £5,100. It was demolished in 1973 and a new church was opened in Tantany Lane. The site now adjoins the local college with the headquarters of the West Bromwich Building Society, occupying most of the land and that of the two neighbouring properties formerly to the right of the church on the corner of Dartmouth Street.

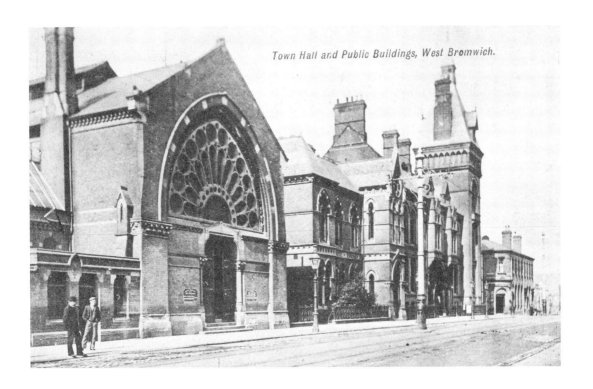

Town Hall and Public Buildings, West Bromwich.

8. The Town Hall was erected in 1875 on part of the Lodge estate that belonged to the Izon family of ironfounders. It was designed in an Italian Gothic style and constructed in brick and stone. The Market Hall to the left, completed in 1874 with Saturdays as market day, was not a commercial success as people preferred to use the more traditional markets higher up the town. The Hall was demolished after 1899 and the land used for the erection of a public library.

9. The High Street's public library was described by that doyen of architectural historians, Pevsner, as 'monumental but not large'. This Carnegie building was opened in 1907 on the market hall site (see previous card). Gas was used to illuminate the library's exterior as part of a West Bromwich Civic Week. The use of gas served to remind local people that they once had the largest works in the kingdom (see card 77). The gas in this case, February 1927, was however supplied from the town's own works – the Swan Village works had long since been bought up by Birmingham Corporation to supply the city, though Wednesbury and other outlying areas were also supplied.

10. The development of culture and education within the town was stimulated in 1886 by the foundation of the West Bromwich Institute in Lodge Road. Its art school eventually became the Ryland Memorial School of Art while the Municipal Science and Technical School was replaced by the Kenrick Technical College. More changes in further education led to an enlarged establishment until still more mergers resulted in today's Sandwell College. The third storey of the Institute was removed in 1976 after a fire.

11. Land at the rear of the Town Hall was initially used for the erection of other public buildings. The remainder of the Lodge estate was developed as a residential area as is seen in this turn of the century card. On the right is the rear section of the Ryland Memorial School of Art to which further building was added next to 77 Edward Street. The shop at the bottom and the buildings to the right on Dartmouth Street have since gone.

West Bromwich Hospital

12. This plain red brick building was among the earlier works of the architects William Martin and John Chamberlain. This Birmingham partnership was later in much demand during the City's period of municipal building. The District Hospital was erected 1869-71 having been predated by a dispensary on the High Street which catered chiefly for out-patients (see card 19). Over a hundred years later the last 33 patients were transferred on 24th November 1979 to the new Sandwell District Hospital at Lyndon. In August 1981 a fire destroyed part of the derelict Edward Street building only hours before scheduled demolition work. Now a new hospital with an attractive brick façade occupies the site.

13. In 1900 Oxford Road was 'described as a proposed new road' that linked Izons Road to Oak Lane. A map of 1902 shows houses on the right between Allen and Chapman Streets and on the opposite side just past the second telegraph.

OLD OAK HOUSE, WEST BROMWICH.

14. Probably West Bromwich's best known building, the Oak House, has amazingly to visitors survived as an architectural gem – a timber-framed yeoman farmhouse in an industrialized urban environment. This Jaysee series postcard shows the house that was restored and presented as a museum to the town through the generosity of Alderman Reuben Farley. On the fiftieth anniversary of that gift it was decided to reopen the building formally, with appropriate period furniture.

Lodge Estate Schools,
Oak Lane, West Bromwich.

15. Situated in the triangle of Oxford, Lodge Roads and Oak Lane this school was opened in 1904 to serve the residential development of the former Lodge estate. This card was produced at that time by H.H. Prince. Today it is only a junior and infants school.

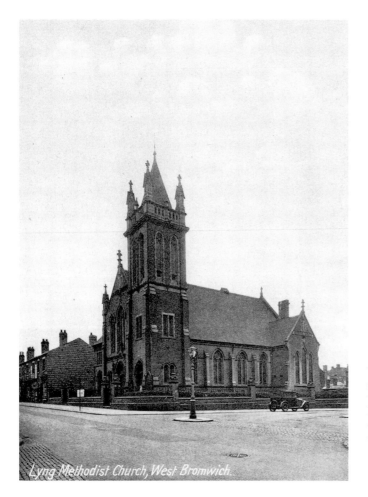

Lyng Methodist Church, West Bromwich.

16. Two Primitive Methodist chapels opened in West Bromwich in 1851. The one on The Lyng was situated in Sams Lane but it became a school when the chapel shown in this card was erected in 1899. In November 1940 enemy bombing destroyed that chapel and so once again the school was used for services. The tower, a local landmark, survived though badly scarred but was demolished to enable road widening in Moor Street. Some twelve years after the air raid a new church was opened.

17. This elevated view, probably from the top of the nearby Lodge Corn Mills, shows Victoria Street bottom left with Price Street swinging round into Paradise Street past the Fire Station tower, now gone as are the distant chimney stacks.

18. A scene from the 1920s in which the characters look almost American, all wearing hats too. The Dudley, Stourbridge & District tramcar No. 53 stands at its St. Michael's Street terminus. The Roman Catholic church was built nearly a hundred years previously and rebuilt in 1877 as a memorial to its first priest, a convert from Anglicanism called George Spencer. He was the youngest son of the 2nd Earl Spencer the great-great-great-grandfather of the present Princess of Wales. Her other local connection is through her stepmother who was previously married to the Earl of Dartmouth. In the background stands the Sandwell public house originally known as the Birmingham House, and on its left the High Street branch of Lye Grant the Reform Street baker.

19. The castellated building adjoining St. Michael's Roman Catholic chapel was originally a private residence before becoming a chemist's shop for a hundred years. It was here that the Provident Medical Dispensary opened in March 1866 and soon proved the need for a general hospital (see card 12). Another forerunner of municipal maturity on this side of the street was the West Bromwich Institution for the Advancement of Knowledge with its reading room and library (see card 9). Next door to Bullus the chemist was 264 High Street, where the gas fitter – a woman called Mrs. Ellen Wright – lived for over 40 years. Across the road for a similarly long period James Freeth kept a coffee shop (today's fish and chip restaurant) adjacent to his grocery business.

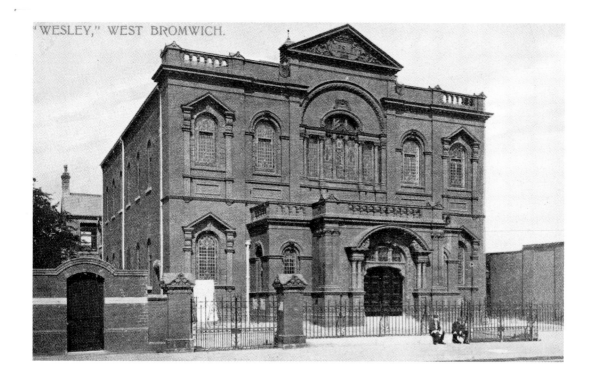

"WESLEY," WEST BROMWICH.

20. This E.S. London postcard franked 1907 shows the Wesley Chapel, High Street, just after the refronting of its façade in 1905-1906. It was demolished in 1972, and another new building opened on the site in 1974. These new premises were shared ecumenically until recently with the Anglicans from Christ Church (see cards 5 and 6).

HIGH STREET, WEST BROMWICH.

21. In this 1930s postcard Galloways the chemist, later Bell & Jones, was for the previous century a draper's shop on the corner of that part of New Street which now forms a section of the Ringway. Although three or four of its neighbours towards the tram remain, most of the buildings on this stretch of the High Street were demolished or rebuilt with the development of the Sandwell Shopping Centre and subsequent pedestrianization. With one or two exceptions the buildings on the right of this High Street scene remain, though they themselves are replacements for the first primitive structures known as 'The Sheds' erected after the enclosure of the common.

NEW STREET, WEST BROMWICH.

22. One of the town's oldest thoroughfares, New Street, has altered radically with today's remnant almost cut off by a linkway and a ringway from the main shopping area. Establishments such as William Morris, the tailor's, seen here on the left at the end of the 1920s, disappeared in the sixties to become the site of the bus station. The barrel shaped front of the billiard hall similar to the one on Handsworth's Soho Road can be seen in the distance close to St. Michael's Roman Catholic chapel. The other buildings as far as Dickens remain but Emmanuel Samuel's Palais de Dance later renamed The Adelphi was destroyed by fire in May 1971.

23. The town centre station was opened in 1854 by the Birmingham, Wolverhampton & Dudley Railway to provide a service between Birmingham and Wolverhampton via West Bromwich. This card was posted in 1911 during Harry Crisp's tenure as station master for the then Great Western Railway. By the 1960s it was an unstaffed halt doomed to closure in 1972.

24. The Dartmouth Square area of the High Street proved popular as a scene for postcards as in this Wrench series production. The Square was developed early in the town's history and was frequently used as a meeting place and was a pitch for both travelling showpeople and iterinant vendors. Later the Salvation Army held services but these and other events caused the police concern because of the obstruction caused by large crowds. Overhead cables and centre poles provide the power for an early open top tramcar.

HIGH STREET, WEST BROMWICH.

25. Behind the fountain was the former Paradise Street where the bakery was erected in 1869 for the shop situated on the apex of the triangle with High Street. The drinking fountain was erected by Alderman Reuben Farley in 1885 as a memorial to his mother. Some 18 years before this an unfulfilled proposal for such a fountain had been made as a memento of the services rendered to the community by local radical and Chartist 'Barber' Wilkes.

DARTMOUTH SQUARE, WEST BROMWICH.

26. Nearly twenty years later this postcard of Dartmouth Square shows some significant changes to the scene in the previous view. The centre poles have been replaced. The fountain has been removed (see card 42) and a clock and underground lavatories have appeared in its place. Bon-Marché, the premises for two drapery establishments, has become a branch of the Birmingham Co-operative Society.

Dartmouth Hôtel,
West Bromwich.
Telephone No. 295.

W. I. Bassett,
Proprietor.

27. This advertising postcard was produced for the hotel that stood on the corner of Spon Lane and Dartmouth Square. In 1834 the 'Dartmouth Arms', was opened on the site of the old 'Bull's Head', originally known as the 'Boot Inn' in the 1750s. The Dartmouth's position in the early development of the town allowed it to assume a special business and social importance – it was used for local courts until 1851. It had a number of licensees closely associated with West Bromwich Albion Football Club as in the case of this card. William Isaiah Bassett, the Albion former player, director, and Club chairman for more than 27 years, held the licence from 1906 until 1920 (see cards 35 and 40). Later another Albion player, Harry Clements, was landlord until his death in 1939. Despite attempts to save it the Dartmouth was eventually scheduled for demolition and the last pints were pulled in February 1977.

28. Among the 29 public houses once found along Spon Lane was this one on the corner of Grice Street, the 'Rusty Lane' of J.B. Priestley's 'English Journey'. The nearby Stour Valley Works provided the name for the pub which was originally just the corner portion – the adjoining higher section was added later by James Reeves whose relatives, the Crees family, continued the business. It closed in 1973 and was demolished for road widening. The beer came from Smethwick's Windmill Brewery which was taken over in 1913 by Mitchells & Butlers.

29. South east of the town the High Street at its Bagnall Street junction becomes the Birmingham Road. At this time, about 1910, tramway overhead cables are carried by poles located down the centre of the road. The trees to the right are part of The Grove Estate described in card 31.

30. A baker's van comes down this street towards High Street and Birmingham Road – the turn on the left seen in the next card. A maid sits on the window ledge of a house on the right – all the houses on that side beyond there have vanished. The large house at the top in Beeches Road still survives despite recent fire damage. The Bagnall family were leading ironfounders at Golds Hill where their works included a school for the children of their employees.

THE AVENUE GROVE CRESENT WESTBROMWICH

31. The Grove was a small estate of four acres of gardens and trees. The actual house still remains but is now known as Trinity House. The Grove's former title, Parkwall, probably and more aptly described its position on the perimeter of Sandwell Park.

32. Sandwell Park Lodge was the entrance to the Earl of Dartmouth's estate. A painting of 1888 shows a driveway straight up to the entry with fencing on either side unlike the slightly ramshackle version of this E.S. London postcard of about 1900. When the 'wonderful stone wall' was demolished to make way for new roads it was found to be brick dressed with stone provoking a local conservationist to comment that 'jerry-building is not just a feature of the 20th century'. Today only the Arch survives almost as a curiosity to the traffic passing it on the junction island above the M5 motorway.

SANDWELL HALL   WESTBROMWICH

33. Sandwell Hall in the above card was rebuilt in 1705 for Lord Dartmouth who had acquired the site in 1701. It had the easily recognizable style of many a Midland mansion erected by William Smith of The Wergs near Tettenhall and his architect/builder brother Francis Smith of Warwick. Previously known as Priory House it had marked the ground on which a Benedictine foundation had been constructed in the 12th century alongside a hermitage and a holy well, hence the 'Sand Well'. In an 1834 directory the Hall was described as 'a beautiful seat in a romantic valley, and so effectually enclosed by a high wall and thick plantations, as to be completely secluded from the busy world that surrounds it'. The Dartmouths had, however, taken a lead in developing coal mining. By 1855 that and other industries were coming too close for aristocratic comfort and the family abandoned the Hall to institutional uses. Eventual demolition came in 1928.

34. This postcard from about 1910 shows the West Bromwich Albion Football Club ground on the left of Halford's Lane. The Hawthorns Hotel on the right was previously known from 1661 as Street House and was the residence of H.H. Halford the ironmaster when it was rebuilt about 1846. Straighthouse Lane was probably the original name for Halford's Lane, and Street House was therefore a corruption. Among its last private residents was Joseph Pearson. Just after the removal of Albion from Stoney Lane to Hawthorns ground in 1900, the public house was granted a license for the refreshment of football spectators. In the centre of the picture are the barn and farm house known as Street House Farm. It was one of the oldest farms in the area extending to some 200 acres and forming part of the Sandwell Park Estate. The buildings survived for two and a half centuries.

Copyright Photo

WEST BROMWICH ALBION F.C., 1930-31.
ENGLISH CUP WINNERS.

Wilkes & Son
West Bromwich

Mr. F. EVERISS, Secretary		RICHARDSON, W.	CARTER	PEARSON	TRENTHAM	SANFORD	F. REED, Trainer
SHAW	MAGEE	RICHARDSON, W. G.	Mr. W. I. BASSETT, Chairman		EDWARDS	WOOD	GLIDDON, Capt.

35. Local photographer Albert Wilkes of 45 Legge Street produced this card of the triumphant team that beat Birmingham City 2-1 to win the F.A. Cup. The season proved a double and unequalled one for Albion because they also won promotion from the Second Division. W.G. Richardson, here seated next to the chairman, scored not only the match-winning goal during a home game against Charlton to clinch promotion but both goals in the Wembley Final.

FORGE FARM · WEST BROMWICH.

36. A farm building that still survives on the edge of the former Sandwell Park Estate is Forge Farm. In this postcard from H. Thompson's 'Glossy Photos' series the scene is little changed today, except that the stream now flows under the road. The farmhouse and land were sold to the local council in the 1920s by the Earl of Dartmouth on condition that it remained unaltered. Its tenant at that time was John Hotchkiss who had previously been the farmer at Sandwell Hall Farm. The 77 acre mixed pig and cattle farm has been worked for more than the past 50 years by the Brown family. Sandwell Council failed recently in its bid to terminate that tenancy as part of a plan to amalgamate the land with that of the nearby Forge Mill Farm interpretation centre.

Swan Pool
WEST BROMWICH

37. What was once the site of Sandwell Mill associated with the nearby Priory was eventually covered by spoil from the Jubilee Pit. Although reduced in size the Swan of Warstone Pool survived as a place where many a person learnt to swim despite the restriction on bathers – the boys here dutifully keep this side of the notice. The display board further on advertises gingerwine by the glass and beer in bottles. This card posted in 1911 was based on a 1907 photograph.

BEECHES ROAD, WEST BROMWICH.

38. Development of Beeches Road, originally 'an ancient horse road' that led to the Three Mile Oak turnpike, took place from the 1860s onwards on what, as the name implies, was a former wooded area at the edge of Sandwell Park. The building behind the now lowered wall was erected 1871-72 replacing the Park Village Sunday School and Chapel to the design of Edward Pincher for the use as a Methodist Chapel. Some of the middle class housing to the left of the chapel have now given way to housing association property.

Eastville = West Bromwich

39. The ultimate in postcard publishing – one of your own house, in this case a view of 51 Beeches Road, produced by High Street photographers, Whitlocks. Two of the owner's sons, Eliot and Geoffrey Spencer, sent festive greetings to friends in Great Barr with a Christmas Eve posting in 1909. Sadly Eliot was to die of war wounds in 1918. His father, the future Sir Harris Spencer, called a significant meeting of Midland industrialists one Sunday morning in this house to sort out the employers' tactics for settling the 1913 metal trades strike (see card 135).

BEECHES RD. WESTBROMWICH

40. In this pre-World War I view of the far end of Beeches Road the pillar box on the corner of Legge Street has gone. The clocktower of Beeches Road School is just visible above the chimneys of a now demolished terrace of houses on the corner of Herbert Street. Between these houses and the clocktower is the roof of St. Philip's Church prior to its extension in 1913-14 for a chancel. On the sunny side is the gateway to no. 85, two doors from which lived William Bassett, sometime West Bromwich Albion player, director, and many years chairman (see cards 27 and 35).

41. This view looking towards the Beeches Road entrance to Dartmouth Park (see next card) was sent on Christmas Eve 1912 to wish season's greetings to its local recipient. Described as a new street in 1869 many of the houses in Herbert Street were erected within the next thirteen years. Children pose between trees that now top the houses. The first building on the right above the Best Wishes is Herbert Cottage dated 1860 next to Hope Cottage of 1878.

West Bromwich, Entrance to Dartmouth Park.
No. 12508

42. This lodge at the Beeches Road entrance to Dartmouth Park stands forlornly today without its railings. Behind it at a lower level is an expressway to take traffic from the M5 motorway and Handsworth that wishes to by-pass the town centre. A partly spiralling footbridge is now the lodge's only means of connection with the rest of the Park. As with the development of so many of the town's public facilities, Alderman Reuben Farley was the moving force that persuaded the Dartmouths to provide the land which he then duly enchanced with suitable structures. Only one of these Farley memorials has survived – the fountain from Dartmouth Square (see card 25) moved to the Park and then back to the pedestrianized area of High Street near to its original position.

Beeches Road School, West Bromwich.

43. A school board was formed in West Bromwich in 1871 and in the same year a by-law was passed making school attendance compulsory. After a few years the town had the best school attendance records amongst the Black Country authorities. Beeches Road School was opened by the Board in 1893 for boys, girls and infants, replacing the Mayer's Green and Queen Street schoolrooms which had been rented for the previous twenty years. This postcard was one of a series from Herbert Henry Prince, a High Street stationer.

44. This splendid looking building in Queen Street was originally intended for use as a public hall. It was completed in 1847 as a Primitive Methodist chapel largely thanks to the munificence of the Spittle family of local coalmasters. This chapel and others in the area (see card 16) were still functioning in the 1930s at the time of union with the Wesleyans and United Methodists. The Queen Street building closed in 1966.

THEATRE ROYAL, West Bromwich.

FOR LOVE AND THE KING
BY C. WATSON MILL.

MONDAY, SEPT. 21st, 1908, for Six Nights.

45. Charles Udall opened a concert hall in Walsall Street for which a licence was granted in 1853. About 1870 it was enlarged and by 1893 it had become the Theatre Royal but two years later there was a disastrous fire. The lessee, James Page Moore, a popular figure who seemed everybody's idea of a theatrical manager, soon had a new building constructed. One wonders what the vicar of Christ Church thought of the female in this publicity postcard, because eight months later he denounced in a sermon the lurid theatrical posters used to promote 'The Sins of a City' at the Theatre Royal.

46. Former Welsh international and 1920s West Bromwich Albion forward Stanley Davies was licensee of the 'Crown & Cushion'. After giving up professional football 'Mr. Versatility' captained West Bromwich Amateurs whose pitch was on the nearby Wasson Fields. Holder's Brewery, founded before 1872, was taken over in 1919 by Mitchells & Butlers Ltd.

Main Entrance, West Bromwich Park.

47. In 1877 some 56 acres of land owned by the Earl of Dartmouth was granted by him at a nominal rent to the town's Improvement Commisioners for the purpose of providing a public park. A year later the grounds were finally opened by the Earl, amid scenes of great excitement and a special fireworks display. The first Park Keeper was Henry Browne who resided in this lodge at the main entrance from New Street.

48. The initial development of Dartmouth Park cost the Improvement Commissioners £6,000. The conservatory and plant house provided the resources for floral displays which were an early feature of the Park's attractions. The nearby 'Crown & Cushion' public house in Lloyd Street took advantage of its side wall to advertise its presence to park visitors.

14513.

Dartmouth Park, West Bromwich

49. Alderman Farley's gift of a bandstand meant that the park band performed on this structure for two afternoons per week during most of the year. Sunday afternoon, however, was reserved for the playing of sacred music. Obviously the attraction of a band provided the opportunity for people to gather, chat or just be seen, as on this Wrench card.

50. There were no crowds on this locally produced view – the premises of the stationers can be seen on card 2.

BAND STAND. DARTMOUTH PARK.
WEST BROMWICH.

51. This card posted in August 1914, just before the start of war, shows the bandstand on a different site. Some twenty years later a new bandstand looking like a miniature Hollywood Bowl with its semi-domed shell for better acoustics was built. People danced in front of it while the band played, but today some concrete steps are the only reminder of those happy times.

Pavilion, West Bromwich Park.

52. The family in the above card posted in July 1910 seems to have the Pavilion to themselves, save for somebody in the upper window – perhaps the marble bust of the Earl of Dartmouth placed in this observatory. The central position of the Pavilion allowed visitors to have commanding views of Sandwell Hall and beyond to Barr Beacon. Its function as a refreshment room ceased in the late 1970s when the Café closed. The local council then hoped to give it a new life as an arts centre. Just as a new roof was completed a disastrous fire in April 1983 left the building in such state of disrepair that demolition was inevitable. The short young trees surrounding the Pavilion in this postcard are now mature and higher than the structure that once dominated them.

Boating Pool, Dartmouth Park, West Bromwich

53. At the time of Queen Victoria's Golden Jubilee Dartmouth Park was enlarged by the gift of some extra land which allowed for the construction of the above boating lake. The female sender of card 31 should perhaps have posted this card instead, as appropriately she wrote to her friend Eva that 'my cousin & I have got off with two swanky fellows. We have been on the Dartmouth pool with them'.

54. These two children play amid the tree lined avenues probably in the area later taken to accommodate part of the Expressway. This card and the previous one of the boating pool were both produced by Harold Bott of Birmingham's New Street who was described in 1909 as a 'picture post card publisher'.

55. The handover to the town of the freehold of Dartmouth Park was the occasion for a royal visit in June 1923 by the then Prince of Wales (the future Edward VIII and later Duke of Windsor). Watched here by Mayor John Bell the Prince chatted to disabled ex-servicemen who were among the vast crowds gathered in the Park. In his characteristic way the Prince regretted that West Bromwich 'had had such a bad time in regard to unemployment'. High Street cameraman David Murray, who was to go to Australia the following year, was among the 'army of professional and amateur photographers' who recorded this and many other 'remarkable scenes of enthusiasm' throughout the royal day.

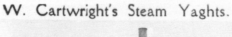

West Bromwich Wakes 1894.

56. The patentee of these steam powered fairground swing boats worked for a time at the Bromford Ironworks in the fitting shop as superintendent. He left this local business to devote himself to the promotion of his invention which soon proved so profitable for him at fairs throughout the country. Not everybody was, however, so pleased with the more substantial steam power – the 'West Bromwich Chronicle' regretted the passing of the manual 'frail-looking boats flashing up and down, while the occupants appeared to be trying to reverse their natural position, and get their feet where their heads ought to be'. By the time of that comment, 1903, the wakes had also lost much of their earlier boisterousness as they developed into fairs of 'comparative quietness'.

The Infirmary, West Bromwich

57. In 1884 an infirmary was added to the existing workhouse administered by the West Bromwich Poor Law Union. This early 1900s postcard was produced by local stationers, Clift Brothers of High Street and Bilhay Street. Improvements to this building were started in 1925 and upon completion three years later a new establishment called Hallam Hospital was inaugurated. The workhouse itself closed in 1937 but some of its buildings survive amid the more recent hospital construction.

58. The three Hadlington brothers started this garage business which also had larger premises since 1904 on the High Street. Eventually in 1976 the Dartmouth Garage was taken over by Charles Clarke in a £300,000 deal. Note the price of petrol – the average cost per gallon dropped from 17½p just after the First World War to 8p in the twenties and thirties before rising again in the period between 1941 and 1944 to 10½p.

WHERE BEER IS SOLD BY THE POUNDE . WEST BROMWICH

59. The closeness of the local pinfold for stray animals to the nearby 'Ring O' Bells' gave rise to this local saying. Although the pound was moved slightly to make way for a road widening scheme, the public house unfortunately was not saved and was demolished in 1971.

OLD CHURCH, WEST BROMWICH.

60. Views of All Saints' Church were published by both local and national postcard producers. This E.S. London card appeared to be the same photograph as that used by H. Thompson. The trees to the left were called the Seven Sisters but have since been removed.

On West Bromwich Road

61. These cottages on Newton Road not far from the 'Scott Arms' backed onto an area known as The Shrubbery. Although they have not survived modern development their then nearest neighbour along the road to West Bromwich, Barr House, still remains in an ivy-clad state.

62. The horse transport heads north up Walsall Road which today is a thoroughfare close to the busy M6 motorway. The three-storey 'Scott Arms' did survive some 180 years until its demolition in May 1966. The old coaching inn gave way to redevelopment with a shopping centre and a replacement opened in August 1968. The original building comprised the inn, a brewery with its own well, and a butcher's shop presumably associated with the cattle market held at the site. An outbuilding was used as the local mortuary while the nearby Roman Catholic chapel owes its origins to services held in the large barn. The inn, its name associated with the leading local landowning family, was the scene of inquests conducted by the neighbourhood magistrate. In 1824 an outbreak of sheep stealing saw the formation of a local Association for the Prosecution of Felons which held its annual dinners at the inn.

The Chapel, Great Barr.

63. Around the time that William Bourne the Hamstead stationer produced this card the Methodist congregation was down five and the Chapel was in danger of closure. By 1916 things were worse with the building becoming dilapidated but soon enough money was raised for repairs. Later new houses in the area would lead to an increase in church membership but the slightly rural aspect of this view, as in the case of the nearby 'Scott Arms', was then gone.

Hamstead Colliery

Nightingale. 132.

64. Hamstead was a sleepy village until experimental borings on local farm land revealed potential coal reserves. The Hamstead Colliery Company Limited was formed and work commenced in June 1875 on sinking a mine. Five years later the first saleable coal was struck at a depth of 573 yards 2 feet. By 1896 some 450 face workers were being employed by the Company. Production continued until March 1965 when geological faults eventually made it uneconomic for the National Coal Board to extract the remaining 20 million tons estimated at the time of closure.

65. Accidents were tragically part of life in local pits but March 1908 at the Hamstead Colliery was particularly disastrous when 25 men were killed. Miners nationwide came to Hamstead to join in the rescue – John Welsby from Yorkshire died attempting to reach the trapped men. His funeral was later attended by 6,000 miners. In 1971 a new local road, Welsby Avenue, was dedicated to his memory.

X SMOKE ISSUING FROM VENTILATING SHAFT.
DIGGING THE TRENCH TO PROVIDE INCREASED VENTILATION.

The Hamstead Colliery Disaster.

ANXIOUS CROWDS WAITING FOR NEWS.

66. While the crowd stood in the rain, the womenfolk of those trapped waited all the time in the engine house, despite a plea from the Bishop of Birmingham to go home and rest. Although houses now cover the Hamstead site, the tragedy and heroism of 1908 will always be remembered.

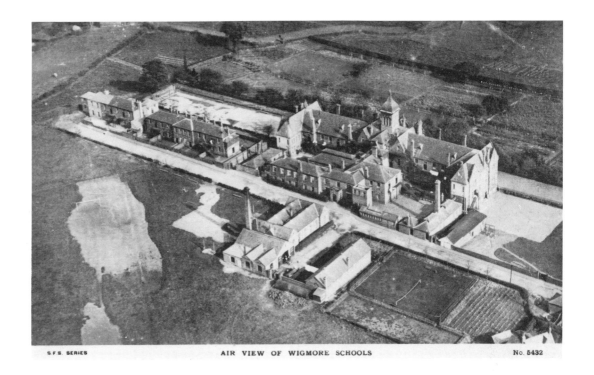

67. Orphaned children from West Bromwich and Walsall attended the schools at Wigmore which despite their then strict regime gained a reputation for enlightened teaching. This institution was closed in 1935 and the buildings in Pennyhill (formerly called Knapenny) Lane served as an approved school, then government and later council offices.

CHARLEMONT CRESCENT. CHARLEMONT. W.B.

68. The sender of this card 'remembered going over the Hall' at the end of the street. Although somewhat shabby looking in this view it was built in the eighteenth century for Jesson Lowe whose family originated in the Lyndon area. During the Sacheverell Riots, Gornet Lowe shot dead two of the mob that attacked the Old Meeting Chapel (see card 78). After the Lowes the Hall passed to their cousins who gave their name to Hallam Street. The Hall's last occupant was a colourful lady from Belgium, the widow of a former Wednesbury town clerk. The house was demolished in 1948. The area was originally called Grumpy's or Grompe's Ground but it remains a mystery why it was changed to Charley Mount as the local hill was once called.

69. Charlemont greengrocer and sub-postmaster Henry Maplethorpe produced a series of postcards in the 1930s. His local views showed his own shop seen here at 106 Hollyhedge Road which was also included on a card that combined five scenes of the area from Stone Cross down to the pound at Church Vale.

The Cemetery — West Bromwich

H. Thompson, Photo

70. In 1858 the West Bromwich Improvement Commissioners purchased for use as a cemetery an area of rising land in Heath Lane near to the old church. This lodge and two chapels in the Gothic style were erected to the designs of a Birmingham architect. Rather macabrely a father writes in 1907 to his daughter 'I send you this picture Post Card hoping you will like it'.

71. Frank Fox was licensee of the old 'Stone Cross Inn' at the time of this postcard in about 1900.
Compared to today's newer public house surrounded by busy roads this scene appeared almost rural
with the neighbouring smithy and sign-cum-lamppost that replaced the original red sandstone cross.

72. On this card published for B.C. Page, of the Bungalow Stores, Charlemont, the 'Stone Cross Inn' has become part of the urban scene, complete with motorcycle and sidecar. The licensee was James Stanton, a former Albion player who had been a half back in the first recorded match on 13th December 1879. For the 1880-1881 season he was elected captain. He also played in Albion's first cup final victory when Stoke was beaten 3-2 on 21st April 1883. Stanton had his own brewery in Braybrook Street until he sold the inn to Darby's Brewery Ltd. in 1928.

73. In Hall Green Road stands a mediaeval timber framed hall surrounded by a moat. This is the Manor House which was restored 1957-1961 after the derelict property had been acquired by the then West Bromwich Corporation. The oldest part is considered to date from about 1300. It was linked to the lordship of the manor until 1823 when the Earls of Dartmouth bought the manorial rights. After that date the House was then owned and occupied by various families. Its dilapidated state, seen here with the 18th and 19th century additions, is in marked contrast to the views produced on post-restoration postcards.

The Bandstand, Hill Top Park, West Bromwich.

74. The grounds of a local mansion were laid out as public park. Meyrick House was purchased in 1896 by West Bromwich Corporation with plans to adapt it for further use. It was however demolished and a Police Station and a reading room, now the branch library, were erected on the site. Although the bandstand has gone the park was increased in size by an additional four acres nearly thirty years ago.

Council Schools, Hill Top, West Bromwich.

75. This school building opened in 1911 with facilities for seniors, juniors and infants, and some three years later it was enlarged. More recently the school concentrated on senior pupils becoming in 1969 Hill Top High School. The family firm of ironmongers, Humphrey Lugg Ltd., has operated next to the school site since the 1890s, having moved from premises in the former Hawkes Lane opposite.

76. Black Lake has its origins in the fourteenth century but by 1820 there was 'continuous settlement along the west side of the main road'. Among the trees in the middle of this card, just above the bridge over the Ridgacre branch canal, was Black Lake House. Cables can be seen stored in the corner of the electricity works that West Bromwich Corporation originally started for the supply of power to the town.

77. Swan Village once had the largest gasworks in the United Kingdom, one tower of which can be seen here beyond where the railway crossed the road. Most of the foreground shows the roof of Black Lake School which closed down in 1969.

78. Religious nonconformity had an eventful history in the area and no more so than at Oakwood where a movement called the Old Meeting (hence the street name), later Ebenezer Church, built the chapel in 1839 seen on the left in this postcard. A former chapel was converted into day and Sunday schools and later rebuilt in 1906 as seen here. An even earlier chapel had been burnt down by mobs inspired by that High Church cleric Henry Sacheverell. A more peaceful association came later in 1875 with the start of the Pleasant Sunday Afternoon Movement founded here by John Blackham. Eventually the Ebenezer joined with the West Bromwich Congregationalists and the building re-opened in 1974 for Hindus as Shree Krishna Temple.

OAKWOOD PARK · WEST BROMWICH

79. The Jesson family lived at a house called Oakwood which had been built in the seventeenth century on a site known as Oakley's Croft. In 1912 the Rev. Thomas Jesson presented the house to the Borough Council. The grounds seen above in this early 1930s postcard adjoin the Jesson Playing Fields but while most of the trees remain, the pavilion and drinking fountain have gone. The house itself was demolished in 1955.

80. Carter's Green at the lower end of West Bromwich's High Street is dominated by the clock tower erected as a tribute to Alderman Reuben Farley within his own lifetime. Just to the rear right can be seen the premises of William Lemon Somers & Son, auctioneers at the Green for over forty years. Two doors away with the blind down was Walter Brooks Williams, the grocer.

FARLEY CLOCK TOWER, WEST BROMWICH.

81. Another view of the Farley Clock looking towards Dudley shows the Wesley Chapel built in 1875-76 on the site of the 'notorious concert hall' called the 'Junction Inn'. The area had an even more gruesome history – a time when they buried suicides by the crossroads at the old Green with a stake through the heart! The chapel was closed by 1949 but was used as a warehouse for some years before demolition in 1970. The sign for Gregory & Tomkins indicates the firm of Joseph George Tomkins, the printer, who by 1912 had premises in the High Street (see card 3).

82. In this view from the top of the Farley Clock, the drapery business of Mary Cook is seen next to Harry Wallett's newsagency on the north side of Carter's Green. While this latter shop is still a newsagent's, the post office has moved further down near to today's traffic island. The post office building photographed here and William Herbert's adjoining corn and seed stores have now disappeared.

THE TOWER CINEMA.   CARTERS GREEN, WEST BROMWICH.

83. The thirties were the era of the super-cinema built with a faint air of the art deco style to incorporate a high standard of luxury and large seating capacity. The Tower at Carter's Green with its 2,000 seats was in this category to such an extent that its local competitors jealously nicknamed it 'The Bloody Tower'. It was opened on Monday 9th December 1935 with a local girl as the star attraction in Hitchcock's unsurpassed version of 'The Thirty-nine Steps'. She was Madeleine Carroll, born in West Bromwich, who became a leading lady of the thirties and forties. The cinema survived like many of its counterparts until the late sixties when it succumbed to the bingo boom. Later the Bingo and Social Club closed and after demolition the site was redeveloped.

84. John, Mary and Thomas Harris successively kept this tavern in Greets Green Road for a period of about sixty years. Puddlers from the adjoining Eagle Iron Works quenched their thirst in the 'Fox and Goose'. The building seen here in about 1911 was later replaced by newer premises.

WESLEYAN CHURCH GREETS GREEN

85. This Methodist chapel on the corner of Ryders Green Road and Greets Green Road was built in 1873 to replace an earlier building of 1835, there being a 'meeting' in the area by 1821. The Wesleyan School to the rear on the right has a stone dated 1856. All the houses in this card posted in 1906 have since been demolished.

Bowling Green, Farley Park, Great Bridge

86. Alderman Reuben Farley had such an 'abiding affection for the place of his birth (Whitehall Road) and one expression of it was his gift of Farley Park'. Apart from the bowling green seen in this 1925 card an entrance lodge and a public reading room, both over to the left, were also provided. The houses on the right in the background stood on the site of the disused Whitehall Colliery.

87. Although there appeared to be a need for a church in the Greets Green area not enough money could be raised to erect a building on land offered by John Bagnall & Sons. Another fifteen years were to elapse before the above stone building was consecrated in 1858 on another site offered as a gift. Similar difficulties were experienced over the erection of a vicarage. During the initial years of his incumbency the Rev. Henry Jesson lived at 32 Fisher Street (see card 91) before moving to the new vicarage which he largely paid for himself.

88. In 1911, when this card, produced in Blackpool, was posted, the Venetian Gothic style national school had been transferred to the control of the local council. It continued in use until 1932 on its site between the church and Farley Park, which is now occupied by the church hall built in 1966, a hundred years after the school had opened.

Stᵗ PETER'S ✝ CHURCH, W.B
Festival, ✝ MAY, 1, 1921.

89. Church festivals in May were a common feature of life in the 1920s, a difficult time for many in the area as the post-war depression began. The local vicar, the Rev. Frank Smith, probably the figure beyond the tree, exhibited his true socialist principles by giving money from concerts straight to the poor before it could be used to purchase items for the church. Most of the properties seen here have disappeared with the exception of the 'Royal Oak' by street lamp and adjoining nos. 259 and 257 Whitehall Road.

"COPHALL" HOTEL OUTING TO CLAVERLEY

90. Joseph Taylor was licensee at the time of this outing from the public house in Sheepwash Lane. There had only been five previous publicans since the 1830s when Joseph Haynes began as a beer retailer. Atkinson's Aston Park Brewery, founded in 1855, survived as an independent company until the Mitchells & Butlers take-over, 104 years later.

91. This postcard locally produced from premises in Great Bridge shows Fisher Street at the turn of the century. Today all these houses have been replaced by two storey blocks of flats between which trees have been planted. The house at the end carries various soap advertisements including one for Hudson's dry soap. Robert Spear Hudson, the West Bromwich High Street chemist, perfected dry soap (today's washing powder). His invention made him a fortune with one local factory and another in Liverpool. When Lever Brothers purchased the business, production was concentrated at the latter works. The shop next to the street lamp was probably at this time the premises of Rachel Burton.

Great Bridge Street, Great Bridge.

92. This 1930s shot shows on the right The Whitehall Cycle Co. which was run for a number of years by James Roberts. The building with five windows on each of the upper storeys consisted, in this view and still today, of three separate premises – a furniture dealer's, a bank, and a social club nearest to the camera. Next to it but set back at an angle was a commercial hotel, the 'Waggon & Horses'. This and the other building towards and including the cycle shop have been demolished. On the opposite of the street can be seen a statuette up on a building that would have been The Palace Cinema which operated for fifty years until its closure in 1960 and eventual demolition.

Great Bridge Street, Great Bridge

93. The road towards Swan Village shows the view the other way to that seen in the previous card. 'The Stork', first on the right, was thought to have been an old coaching inn with evidence of stabling at the rear where there was also a bowling green. Next door was a barber's and a fancy goods shop owned for long periods by two families – the widow in each case seemed to take on the late husband's business. Adjacent at no. 68 was the local branch of the grocery multiple, George Mason, a nationwide concern that had its origins in West Bromwich. 'The Lion Inn' further along was run for many years by Charles Lucas, described as a beer retailer. Eventually G. Hipkins, the pork butcher at nos. 60-64, extended its premises replacing its neighbours with a meat products factory that towered over 'The Stork' but demolition has now claimed both of them. The other side of the street from the Post Office down to no. 49 has fared much better with refurbishment to many properties.

NEW ROAD GREAT BRIDGE

94. This lively scene is full of detail – the horses and carts have a more heavy and business-like look to them than those seen in other cards throughout this book. This card was produced (probably about 1900) by Blackham the stationers, seen here on the right – 'post cards' clearly advertised on the window! This business and the grocers next door (both actually Market Place addresses) were still trading forty years later. Today the railway bridge (carrying the Great Bridge Branch line of the Great Western Railway Co.) is gone as is the building, 120 New Road, next to the Union Supply Co. Ltd.

Market Place, Great Bridge.

95. This Wrench card shows Blackham's neighbours on the road towards West Bromwich. Thomas Alfred Collins ran his boot and shoe making business here at nos. 7 and 8 for about twenty years before expanding with branches, so that in 1904 there were three shops in Wolverhampton and six others throughout the Black Country.

15057

Street and Post Office, *Great Bridge*

96. Quite a group of children line up outside the corner premises of Purser Bros. for this Wrench view. As the correspondence side of the card has been overprinted by Blackham's to publicize stocks of Christmas cards and presents it would seem to indicate that the Great Bridge stationer had probably a quantity of these postcards after the failure of the Wrench business and had proceeded to give them away as a free advertising promotion for his own firm.

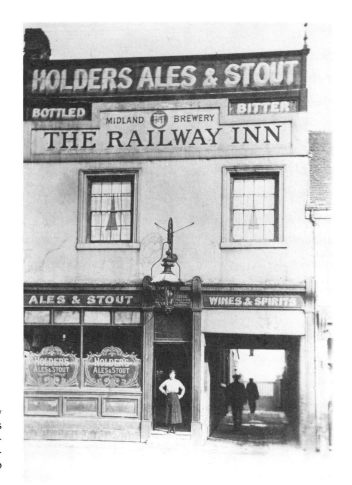

97. The side passageway provided access from New Road to one of the two Great Bridge stations – in this case the L. & N.W.R. South Staffordshire Line. William Pearson was licensee but it was Mitchells & Butlers beer – Holder's Midland Brewery was close to Birmingham's Curzon Street station.

"Great Bridge Rd, Tipton"

William Haddon, Publisher, Tipton

98. Although a local publication this card was printed in Germany. The impressive post office built in Victorian times on the corner of Horseley Road is the sole survivor of the buildings on the left. The first three buildings on the right have gone as well as some others further down the road towards Great Bridge.

99. Thomas Edward Smith who had these shops during the 1920s and 1930s was probably the same grocer with premises in Sedgley's Dudley Road. While not all buildings along Horseley Heath survive today (see previous and next card) these remain unaltered on the upper storey.

HORSELEY. HEATH. TIPTON.

100. All the buildings in this view with the exception of the three nearest to Dudley Port station have disappeared. The high vantage point used by the photographer had obviously attracted the attention of passers-by in this postcard produced by the Horseley Press.

The Canal Burst at Dudley Port. 9th Sept. 1899.

101. A dramatic canal burst occurred in the early hours of a Saturday morning in September 1899 close to the railway line between Dudley Port and Albion stations. Damage estimated at £50,000 was not only caused by the 100 yard break in the Birmingham Canal but the escaping water quickly filled the local brickworks' claypit, itself 100 yards deep, and flooded about three acres of surrounding land. Miraculously no one was injured. Thousands of sightseers visited the scene which also attracted many photographers.

Tividale Church.

102. The greenhouse and other outbuildings of houses in Tividale Road once adjoining St. Michael's Church are clearly visible in this card produced by William Haddon of Tipton. The church was built in 1877-1878 after an ecclesiastical parish was formed from parts of Tipton and neighbouring Rowley Regis.

The Library, Tipton

PUBLISHED FOR J. BOOTH

103. Architectural historian, Nikolaus Pevsner, described the Library as 'quite a spectacular building compared with what else Tipton has to offer'. It was designed by George Wenyon in an Arts and Crafts Movement style and opened in 1906 – a gift from Andrew Carnegie, the universal benefactor of public libraries. This card was 'published for' probably Jonas Booth, a Dudley Port newsagent.

VICTORIA PARK, TIPTON.

104. It was some eight years from the suggestion for a public open space in Tipton to the actual inauguration on 29th July 1901 of Victoria Park, so named in commemoration of the Diamond Jubilee of Queen Victoria. The chosen 34 acre site was previously derelict but covered in the evidence of its former use as a mining area – a large mound estimated at over 60,000 tons which was then moved. Waterproofing of the lake proved difficult. Some of the 15,000 trees and shrubs planted can be seen in the foreground of this postcard produced by local printers, Elton & Brown of Canal Street.

Tipton's War Memorial, Unveiled by Marquis of Cambridge.

105. In 1921 the Marquis of Cambridge who himself served as an officer in World War I, came to Victoria Park to unveil the obelisk. The memorial also commemorated the names of those who died in Union Street during a Zeppelin raid. J.E. Willisford was the photographer for this card which was merchandised by the Horseley Press.

ENTRANCE TO VICTORIA PARK, TIPTON.

OWEN STREET, TIPTON.

106. In the top part of this double view the park superinten-dent's house is shown on the left while the other houses are on the far side of Victoria Road (formerly Randle's Lane) and in between is a distant view of the Gas Works which opened in 1882. Below, the 'Albion Inn', Metropolitan Bank House (where the sender of this John Price & Son's Real Photo Series postcard was staying in 1911), and other buildings along this side have been replaced by a shopping precinct linked to similarly red bricked housing (see next card for a view from the opposite end of the street). On the other side the corn merchants (probably William & Samuel Foster) have gone. The adjoining bank has been super-seded by newer premises but the third building also a bank remains alongside the setback St. Paul's Church.

"Owen Street, Tipton"

William Haddon, Publisher, Tipton

107. This busy street scene at the turn of the century – the epitome of a Black Country town's main street – looks quite different today. Modern residential housing has been carefully constructed in red brick to form a conservation area replacing the 'Cow and Calf' and shops. The 'Fountain Inn', associated with the Tipton Slasher, William Perry, champion prize fighter 1850-1857, was restored in 1984 as one of the Black Country's most famous public houses.

WESLEYAN CHURCH, PARK LANE, TIPTON.

108. 'This is my Church' wrote the sender of this card produced by local confectioner, Ellis A. Billingham. Others gave it the more grand title of 'Tipton's Methodist Cathedral'. This was, however, the third building on the Tipton Green site where the first Wesleyan Preaching House was erected in 1750. A fourth chapel costing £65,000 was opened on 1st July 1978 providing accommodation for a combination of three congregations – Park Lane itself plus Bell Street and Bloomfield Methodists.

Dudley Road. Tipton

109. The housing on the left with the exception of three dwellings opposite the vicarage have all been replaced by recent redevelopment. The substantial middle class houses either side of St. Matthew's Church remain. The parsonage house seen in the middle of this view was built in 1884. This card posted in 1907 was produced by local printers, Elton & Brown of Canal Street.

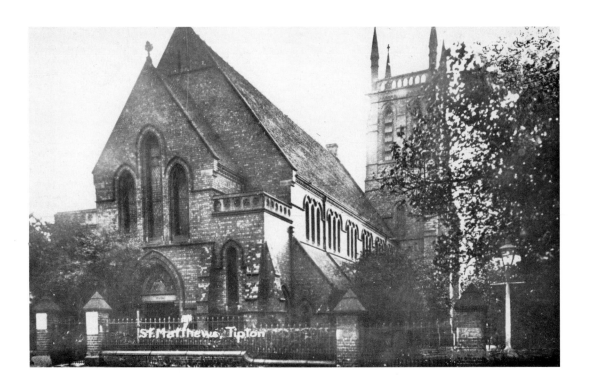

110. This close-up 'Real Photo' postcard shows the Dudley Road church erected in 1880 at a then cost of £5,903. Its architect, J.H. Gibbons, designed it in the Early English style.

Castle Road, Tipton.

111. Just two roads up on the right from St. Matthew's (of the last two cards) is Castle Road first known as Quarry Lane. The field in this card dated 1914 has been built over but these houses from 'The Gables' on the left remain unaltered. Only in the gap on the far right is a newer house.

MUNICIPAL BLDS TIPTON

112. Full local government was late coming to Tipton which only in 1938 received its Royal Charter granting non-county borough status. These municipal offices, originally industrial buildings, were opened in March 1935 with a 200 foot frontage on Sedgley Road West. Interestingly for the time reinforced concrete was used. The 1966 Black Country local government re-organization saw boundary changes and these premises became an annex for Dudley Technical College. The nearby railway bridge carried the G.W.R. Oxford, Worcester & Wolverhampton Line with its Tipton Station at this point while the other Tipton Station on the L. & N.W.R. Stour Valley Line survives at Owen Street.

ON THE CANAL, BLOOMFIELD, TIPTON.   635.

113. On this John Price & Sons 'Real Photo' that looks from Factory Bridge towards St. Matthew's Church and Dudley Castle hill in the far distance, only the stables in the centre of these canalside buildings have survived. The cowl of the malthouse at the end of the row is just visible above the roof of the stables – there was a number of malthouses in the Bloomfield area. A plaque from the Birmingham Canal Navigation Society commemorates the renovation of the Victorian period stables under local council supervision of a government Manpower Services Commission scheme.

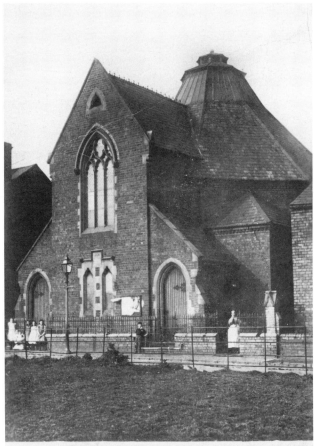

TABERNACLE, REGENT ST. PRINCES END
BUILT 1856. DEMOLISHED 1929.

114. Methodism's New Connection built this place of worship as an off-shoot of Tipton's Canal Street Chapel. A nineteenth century journalist wrote: 'Its architecture is somewhat pretentious, the polygonal formation of its glazed roof giving it an interior in the form of an amphitheatre.' For this card posted in 1931 he continued rather prophetically: 'It is doubtful, whether, in the interests of economy, such a construction is suitable to the Black Country.'

115. This was the original parish church for Tipton until St. Martin's moved in the late eighteenth century to Lower Church Lane (see next card). Rebuilding took place in 1854 and it was then dedicated to St. John. Later local mining operations caused such damage to the church that it closed for a short period between 1913 and 1921. This view was a John Price & Son's Picture Post Card.

St. John's Church, Prince's End, Tipton.

The Tower of this, the most ancient building in Tipton, was restored in 1682, but the foundation of the church, according to Domesday Book, was laid in the year 680 or thereabouts.

No.4.

ST MARTIN'S PARISH CHURCH, TIPTON

116. Known locally as the 'Pepper Pot' this domed bell tower was removed during restoration in the sixties. The church was built in the eighteenth century as a replacement for an earlier parish church. John Keyte of Kidderminster, the 'able architect' who had two years previously refitted Tewkesbury Abbey Church, is credited with the design for Tipton. The terrace across the road has disappeared with the exception to the far left in this postcard of the 'Old Court House' public house.

117. The first ever royal visit to Tipton suffered from a few organizational hiccups because local officials had no experience with such events. This postcard wrongly titles Princess Marie Louise of Schleswig-Holstein – Aribert was her husbands name – as 'H.R.H.' instead of 'H.H.', the last British princess to bear the style of Highness. The Princess was actively interested in the work of Queen Alexandra's nurses. Local subscriptions and contributions raised enough money within a year of the formation of the Tipton Nursing Association for the opening of this building, now demolished, in Lower Church Lane.

118. The weather was 'gloriously bright and fine' for the visit to Tipton by Princess Marie Louise. The royal procession is seen here at the start of its route in Owen Street just about to pass the 'Albion Inn'. Some local lads gained a good vantage point to watch by standing on the window ledges of the then Council Building, which was later to become a fire station until the brigade moved in 1971 to its present site in Alexandra Road.

119. This Blackham postcard despatched in 1904 shows people taking advantage of the shade from the trees along the approach to the central spire of the two chapels – Church of England to the left and Nonconformist to the right. The site near Horseley Farm was acquired in 1871. Wrench had produced a similar view with more of the lodge visible but captioned 'Toll End Cemetery, Great Bridge'. Blackham overprinted the correspondence side with their own advertising and then issued presumably their own card correctly titled.

MOAT FARM.

OCKER HILL.
DICKINSON

120. Some of Tipton's original farms survived as working units into the early part of this century such as this Moat Farm, which was the home farm to the nearby Walker's Hall. While the farmhouse was over 200 years old it was thought that some of the timber framed outbuildings dated possibly from the fourteenth century.

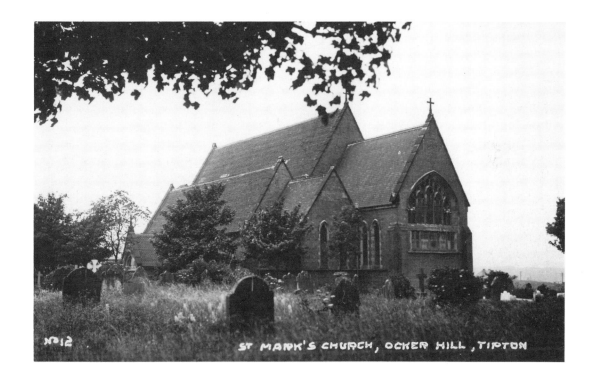

St Mark's Church, Ocker Hill, Tipton

121. As Ocker Hill with its network of canals was nicknamed the 'Venice of the Midlands' it seemed appropriate that the church consecrated in November 1849, was dedicated to St. Mark. Built in a decorated Gothic style using hard blue bricks it was intended to include a tower and steeple, but local mining conditions prevented such a plan.

122. Amazingly the shed-like printer's premises survive today as a newsagent's. The Ocker Hill Junior School in the background has been replaced by a smaller modern structure. The outbuilding behind the tram and the 'Crown & Cushion' remain unaltered. The faint Station Bridge caption on this view of about 1905 refers to the then L. & N.W.R. Princes End Branch railway line that ran through the area.

KING'S HILL PARK WEDNESBURY.

123. The men and boys on this card all strike a similar pose – hands in pockets, note all wear flat caps – taken from Darlston Road. Although the pillars have been reduced in height the iron gates survived the war effort. King's Hill Park, converted out of a pit mound and waste land, was opened in October 1900 but more recent boundary changes resulted in its coming under the jurisdiction of Walsall Borough Council.

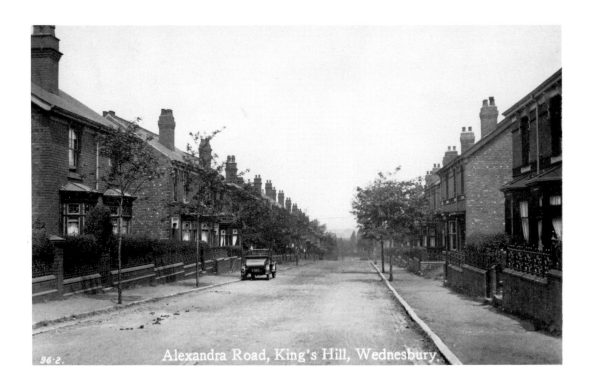

Alexandra Road, King's Hill, Wednesbury.

96·2.

124. On a local map of 1901 this road appeared as an unnamed outline for development and nos. 10-11, Ryton Cottages, just beyond the car on the left bear the date 1906. To the south of this street was the oddly titled firm 'The Steel Nut' and Joseph Hampton Ltd. The card was produced by B.D. Smith, newsagent and stationer, of nearby Walsall Road. This copy was posted obviously some years after publication by someone in New York to an address in San Francisco!

Wednesbury from King's Hill Road

125. How much of the land around Wednesbury remained unbuilt upon even in 1905 is shown in this Valentine card. Old Park Road leading from King's Hill is seen here swinging round to Hall End – it was later straightened. To the far left of the churches beyond the tall presbytery part of the old manor house survived until about this time.

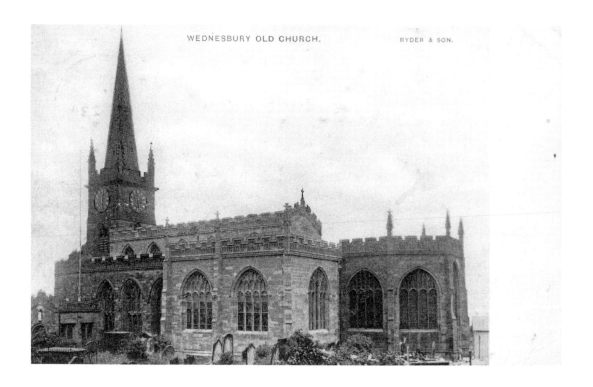

126. St. Bartholomew's stands high on its hill overlooking the town centre of Wednesbury. The church's interior contains an unusual lectern that dispenses with the customary eagle – instead a fighting cock complete with spurs reminds us of the 'cruel sport' so long a tradition of the region.

St. Mary's Catholic Church, Wednesbury. The Presbytery.

127. The Anglicans share the same hill with St. Mary's Roman Catholic Chapel built in brick in 1873-1874. Both churches overlook Ethelfleda Terrace, a name commemorating the connection with the Mercian princess daughter of King Alfred who in her time established across the Midlands a series of fortifications that included Wednesbury, Tamworth, and the future splendour of Warwick Castle. The same architect, Gilbert Blount, probably designed the Presbytery as well as the Chapel.

128. The Market Place is full for this Wednesbury & District Co-operative Society's Children's Gala in the early 1920s. The shop on the corner of Spring Head just by the tramway pole is still a Co-operative Store but some of the other buildings such as the 'Golden Cross' and the butchers have been rebuilt. The clock tower was erected by public subscription to commemorate George V's coronation in 1911. The bank and other buildings towards Lower High Street have been little altered.

Market Place, Wednesbury

129. About 20 years before the Gala in the previous card something back along the tramway was attracting the attention of most of the men and boys in this view. The hosiery and hat business at no. 13 was first run for twenty years by Luke Benton Longmore and then by Frederick William Longmore. Neighbouring shop, Craddock Bros., was the local branch of the Staffordshire boot and shoe makers. Across the street was the coffee house owned by the Staffordshire Cafe Co. Ltd., which had six other establishments in Wolverhampton, Bilston, and Dudley.

130. Ryder & Son, publishers of the 'Wednesbury Herald', seem to have had a virtual monopoly in the production of views of the town. A sign hanging here on the right indicates their former premises at 12, Spring Head but even today no. 13 also survives as Ryder's Chambers. Behind the lady with the pram the imposing Methodist Chapel on the corner of Wharfedale Street is now a car park, but the building just in the picture across the street on the left while still belonging to the Methodists, was used as a Sunday school – the newer present chapel adjoins it. No. 5 has now lost its Dutch style gabling. At the top in Walsall Street is the Conservative Club opened in October 1904 by Lord Windsor on the site of Spring Head House.

131. The organ at the centre of this interior cost £603 while the chapel, the second to be built in 1867 for Spring Head methodists required nearly £4,000. The chapel's impressive exterior can be seen in the Ryder & Son postcard of Spring Head looking towards Walsall Road (see previous card).

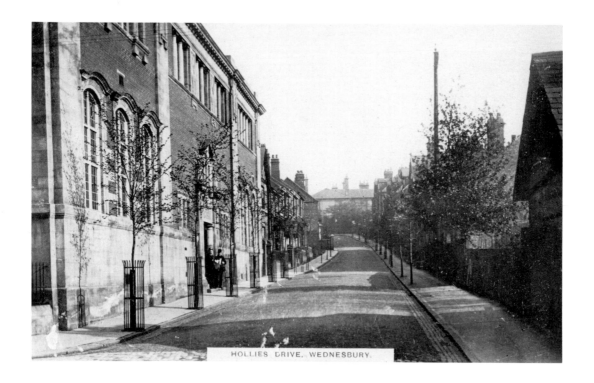

HOLLIES DRIVE, WEDNESBURY.

132. On the corner of Hollies Drive is the 1908 public library which Pevsner described as 'the best secular building of Wednesbury'. Opposite in 1926 a garden of remembrance would be dedicated. At the top of the road stood 'The Hollies', a curious gothic looking building to which James Russell had added battlemented walls and towers in the grounds.

Lodge in Wednesbury Park.

RYDER & SON

133. Brunswick Park opened in the year of Queen Victoria's Jubilee, 1887, on a site covering 24 acres that included a pit mound. This seemingly unattractive feature was however pleasantly landscaped with trees and was the vantage point from which this view was taken. The card posted in 1906 shows houses in Wood Green Road, nos. 2 to 5 and 6 (appropriately named Park Villas). The wooden-like gates were replaced by fuller iron ones and the flowerbeds and mound of bushes to the left are now the domain of tall trees.

WOOD GREEN RD
WEDNESBURY
PRICE'S SERIES

134. Nos. 13-24, Wood Green Road feature in this card probably produced by the Wednesbury stationer, R. Price. Brunswick Park opposite is more open today – the railings have disappeared but the gate posts near the second tramway pole are still a reminder of the park's previous dignity. In the distance is the spire of St. Paul's, a church built and paid for by the Elwells as their own family memorial, an indication of the wealth and influence of these owners of Wednesbury Forge. In front of the spire in the middle of the card is The Limes, one-time residence of Mrs. Edwin Richards the Art Gallery's benefactress (see card 138) but now part of Sandwell College.

STRIKERS DEMONSTRATION JUNE 16 1913

135. Workers at the Crown Tube Works of John Russell & Sons Ltd. went on strike in May-July 1913 and the dispute spread throughout the Black Country involving nearly 37,000 men. Local photographer James Bernard produced this card of the strikers marching down Lower High Street complete with band in their midst.

136. Bridge Street's Drill Hall was erected in 1893 as the headquarters of the Wednesbury detachment of the 2nd Volunteer Battalion of the South Staffordshire Regiment. Facilities included an armoury, officers' and mens' quarters, and a house for the sergeant-instructor as well as the actual hall itself, measuring 88 ft. x 44 ft. complete with spectators' gallery. It continued in use until the 1960s as a training centre for the Territorial Army and the local cadet unit.

137. It seems amazing that Methodism became so strong throughout the Black Country when one considers the area's hostility to Nonconformity (see card 78). John Wesley suffered greatly at the hands of local people who in October 1743 took him forcibly before various magistrates who merely expressed disinterest in the preacher's activities. Muchin's real name was George Clifton and his cottage was pulled down in 1934.

The cross indicates a cottage off Bridge Street, once the home of "Honest Munchin," a converted ruffian who rescued John Wesley from his would-be murderers in the historic Wednesbury riots in 1743. He died at Birmingham in 1789, at the age of 85, and his tombstone may be seen in St. Paul's Churchyard there.

Oct. 1904

Honest Munchin's Cottage, Wednesbury.

Ryder & Son.

Art Gallery and Municipal Buildings, Wednesbury

138. The people on this card stand and pose along a street which today roaring traffic isolates from the rest of the town. The Municipal Offices or Town Hall was constructed just before the start of World War I while the adjacent Art Gallery had been erected over twenty years earlier. The gallery had been built as a result of a bequest in 1895 by Mrs. Richards (see card 134) consisting of a collection of pictures and some £2,000 towards a building to contain the paintings. Ruskin pottery and Wednesbury enamels are among the Gallery's other treasures.

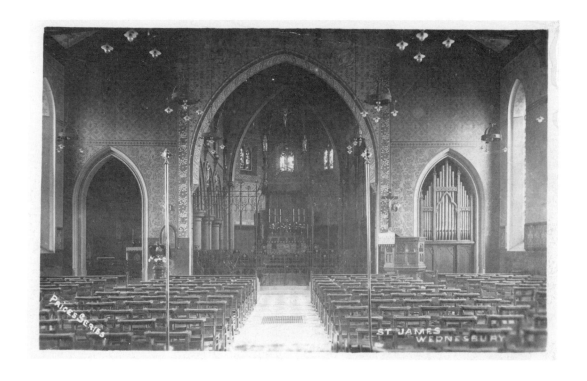

139. This card was posted in 1915 by someone who attended services in the aisleless church. 'Nice isn't it?' she commented to her friend in Suffolk. One of the earlier rectors was the eloquent preacher Richard Twigg, whose religious fervour earned him the nickname 'Apostle of the Black Country'. Notable among the many people affected by his example of devotion to the Christian faith was Dorothy Wyndlow Pattison, better known as Walsall's heroine Sister Dora.

140. Lastly this card is unusual in that its publishers, the Rotary Photographic Co. Ltd., produced numerous 'real photograph' postcard views. It is also something of a further curiousity in that it was posted in August 1917 from West Bromwich to an address in that most famous of picture postcard resorts, Blackpool. The sender wished the addressee 'a very pleasant Bank Holiday'!